TRAIPSING FROM A LANCASHIRE TOLL BAR:

Bretherton, Croston, Hesketh Bank,
Hoole, Tarleton & Walmer Bridge
in focus

Betty Gilkes & Stan Pickles

C000164644

Landy Publishing 2005

ISBN 1 872895 65 4

A catalogue record of this book is available from the British Library.

Layout by Sue Clarke
Printed by Nayler the Printer, Accrington. Tel 01254 234247

Landy Publishing have also published:-

Bolland Forest & the Hodder Valley by Greenwood & Bolton
Northward by Anthony Hewitson
Preston in Focus by Stephen Sartin
Penwortham, Hutton & Longton in Focus by Catherine Rees
Glimpses of Glasson Dock and Vicinity by Ruth Z. Roskell

A full list is available from:-

Landy Publishing
"Acorns" 3 Staining Rise, Staining, Blackpool, FY3 0BU
Tel/Fax 01253 895678

INTRODUCTION

This book came about through the publisher acquiring a collection of picture postcards and giving us the opportunity to study and write about them. The finished book is a sequel to one compiled by Catherine Rees on neighbouring Penwortham, Hutton and Longton. This time the reader has the chance to visit **six** country villages on a leisurely amble – a *'traipse'* in old Lancashire talk – which we have grouped into three short journeys centred around the toll bar, which was for so long a focal point in the area on which we – as did the early photographers – focus.

The writing of the book has been a pleasure, primarily because it has brought out latent interests for both of us, but particularly because we have had the willing assistance of so many people – many of whom are more knowledgeable in their particular field than us.

Amongst those who have been most helpful and generous with their time, and in some instances giving ready permission to use their own material, are Kathleen Almond, Jean Aughton, Sylvia Birtles, Alice Bonney, David Burney and family, Geoffrey Coxhead, Ron Critchley, Julie Donnelly, Lizzie Ellison, Keith Farrington, Alice Hewitson, Frank Hewitson, William Hunter, Gerald Iddon, David and Joan Johnson, Mona Lewis, Jean Norris, Jane Pickles, Maria Rae, Sally Rimmer, Jane Riding-Smyth, Jack and Irene Staziker, Beatrice Sumner, Elizabeth Swarbrick, Margaret Taylor, Lynn Higham of the Walmer Bridge Inn, Ann Whalley, Tom and Betty Wignall, Joan Witter and Maggie Wright. We also extend our thanks to those not listed here who have helped in any way and given us snippets of information en route. Especial thanks, of course, go to our own families who have been most supportive and very patient.

In conclusion we would like to dedicate the book to the memory of Linda Taylor of Hoole, a local historian who, sadly, died during the initial period of our research and would have been a fount of information.

Betty Gilkes and Stan Pickles
Walmer Bridge, August 2005

ANNO PRIMO & SECUNDO

GEORGII IV. REGIS.

••

Cap. ciii.

An Act for making the Townships and Hamlets of
Tarleton, and of *Hesketh with Becconsall*, in the
Parish of *Croston*, and Part of the Rectory and
Vicarage thereof, in the County of *Lancaster*,
separate and distinct Parishes. [8th *June* 1821.]

WHEREAS the Parish of *Croston*, in the County Palatine of *Lancaster*, is very extensive, and hath in it one Parish Church called the Parish Church of *Croston*, and the Townships of *Tarleton* and of *Hesketh with Becconsall* respectively are situated within the said Parish, and now form Part of the Rectory and Vicarage thereof, and are distinguished and bounded by ancient and known Limits and Boundaries, and have separate and distinct Overseers of the Poor, and have also separate and distinct Chapels of Ease of the Church of the Parish of *Croston*, and for the Accommodation of the Inhabitants of the said Townships and the Places therein: And whereas the Inhabitants of the said Townships cannot with Conveniency repair to the said Parish Church of *Croston*, by reason of the remote Distance of many Parts of the said Townships from the same, and of the Inundations of Waters happening in those Parts: And whereas the Revenues and Endowments belonging to the Rectory and Vicarage of the said Parish of *Croston* will be sufficient and ample for Three Rectories, for the Maintenance of the Cure of Souls, as well within the said Township of *Tarleton* as also within the said Township

[*Local.*]   35 T   of

All of the villages featured within this publication were at one time within the ancient parish of Croston – "*Cross Town*" – this cross still standing at the entrance to Church Street. The parish formerly comprised the townships of Bispham, Bretherton, Chorley, Croston, Hesketh-with-Becconsall, Mawdsley, Rufford, Tarleton, and Ulnes Walton, also the chapelry of Hoole, consisting of Much Hoole and Little Hoole. As each grew they were, one by one, given independent status under an Act of Parliament similar to this one shown, which in 1821 granted independence to Tarleton and Hesketh with Becconsall. It had been much earlier, in 1641 – during the reign of Charles I – when Hoole, the first of these villages, was given independent parish status and its own rector. With the exception of obvious name changes, the wording of these acts some 180 years apart is virtually identical – including the reference to the *"Inundations of Waters"*.

OLD TOLL BAR, BRETHERTON.

Whilst these villages were once all in the parish of Croston they now strangely form the extremes of three local borough authorities, with the most central and pivotal point for the three being the site of the old toll bar just inside the village of Bretherton.

Following the original Turnpike Act of 1555, by 1663 over 400 separate turnpike acts had appeared on the Statute Books, in order that users of main highways should pay toll, thus helping small or poor parishes with their maintenance. Each site was sponsored by groups of local J.P's and landowners, *"Bretherton Toll Bar"* being one such. The *"Liverpool and Preston Turnpike Trust"* – established in 1771, was dissolved in 1873 and it was later in the 1920's when the road became the A59.

With ever-increasing road traffic and several accidents, mainly to the bowed front wall and window – in some cases the offending vehicle ending up in the front room of the house – the toll bar is no more, the junction having been modified to include a roundabout on the site of the house-cum-shop in the picture.

So it is from this point that we begin our three journeys. As we view this photograph, taken in the 1930's, with our backs to the south-west, Tarleton and Hesketh Bank in the borough of West Lancashire are behind us. To the east lie Bretherton and Croston, in the borough of Chorley; but we begin by travelling north into the borough of South Ribble and to the villages of Hoole and Walmer Bridge.

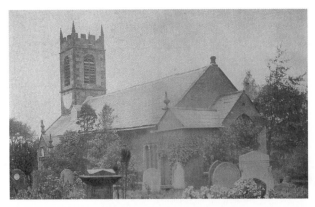

Journeying north from the toll bar, along the turnpike road, the Parish Church of St. Michael has occupied an important part in the life of Hoole from as far back as 1628, when it was built. Significantly since its severance from the mother church of Croston in 1641 (although due to subsequent development and house building, and the fact that a new arterial road divided parts of the village in the 1920's) its position is now to the extreme south western corner of Much Hoole.

Built of Dutch brick by the Stones family of Carr House, Bretherton, serving the parishes of Hoole and Bretherton as chapel of ease to the mother church at Croston, it has seen many changes and additions to its structure, and has received much attention due to its connection with Jeremiah Horrocks, a young astronomer and minister, who in his short life achieved fame by calculating and first observing the transit of Venus across the face of the sun in 1639. On the tower, the sundial, synonymous with the work and witness of Horrocks, is clearly visible. *(For more detailed information on the work and achievements of Horrocks and on the history of the church together with up-to-date contact numbers visit* www.hooleCEchurch.org.uk)

This roadside picture from the early 1900's shows much more foliage on the trees suggesting that it was summertime; could it be that the quartet of elegant churchgoers were attending a wedding? The large gate and gateposts were reduced in height in 1974 when the section of the perimeter wall in the foreground was demolished and re-routed to make way for the present car park, some trees and bushes being removed in the process.

St. Michael's Church, Hoole, Lancs.

The extent of burials in the third picture may indicate that this southern aspect of the church was photographed about 1936; to the extreme left, the pathway leads to the war memorial, paying tribute to 26 men of the village who died in the First World War, a further three names being added following the Second World War.

Through the years many dedicated church members have given freely of their time and talents to keep the building and community in good order, none more so than Thomas Sharples, sexton at the church for 50 years. In reporting his death in February 1907, the "*Preston Guardian*" paid tribute to this dedication, and to the respect in which he was held throughout West Lancashire, and noting that over the years, whilst serving under Revd Robert Brickel and Revd Edmund Dunne (senior), he had officiated at over 1000 funerals – quite an achievement in a small rural village.

Here we can see Mr Sharples posing by the church porch and taking a breather in the churchyard, the tending of which occupied much of his time.

This photograph, taken just a few years before his death, gives a good indication of what the graves and surroundings looked like about 100 years ago – showing a sparseness of trees compared with today, with many graves having railings and glass memorial domes.

In the background to the right of the church can be seen Church Farm, the home of the Wilson family for many years – in fact in the section of the church yard adjacent to the north wall of the church is a grave bearing the Wilson family name and a carved hand with the finger pointing to the farm with the words *"A native of this house"*.

Mr and Mrs Sharples lived in the sexton's cottage known locally as *"Th'owd Thatch"* where earlier they had worked as hand loom weavers, carrying the *'weft'* – the finished product of their labours (which may also have been called *'a piece'*) – to either Preston or Chorley. Following his death, the cottage and his church duties were taken over by Robert Banks, the cottage eventually being demolished in the 1920's to make way for the present A59 road.

In 1850 the Hoole C of E school was built opposite the church. On the left of the picture can be seen the porch / cloakroom, containing rows of coat pegs and a cold water drinking basin, but due to modernisation and extensions this has been demolished, as has much of the school house on the right, only a section of the ground floor being retained, initially for storage then converted for school use.

Note the large but high windows – too high for the children to be distracted by looking out – and apart from these having been lowered, much of this main body of the school still remains and houses two infant classrooms.

The headmaster was Mr James Bonney, pictured here with the teaching staff in the early 1900's – his wife Jane and the Misses Grace and Polly Wiggans.

Moving on to 1927, the new headmaster was Mr. Rymer, pictured here with his class. Left to right, back row – Tom Greenwood, Matt Forshaw, Stanley Oldham, John Gregson, Fred Holden, Bill Wilson; middle row – George Barker, Frank Hewitson, Marjorie Bennett, Maggie Fiddler, Ellen Ball, Eileen Humber, John Bennett; front row – Jane Edmondson, Alice Delves, Daisy Fiddler, Margaret Holden, Agnes Orritt, Joan Humber, Margaret Harrison, Jack Sergeant.

A pre-World War II picture of Miss Grace Wiggans' class in 1936 shows left to right, back row – John Gregson, Derek Wilson, Bob Gregson, Bert Chadwick, Harry Jackson; second row – Dorothy Harrison, Irene Holt, Elizabeth Kirby, Margaret Iddon, Margaret Kirby, Betty Harrison, Phyllis Haskayne; third row – Mary Holt, Muriel Moon, Margaret Maughan, Vera Hague, Alice Taylor, Nelly Gregson; front row – John Bannister, Frank Clark, John Hague, Lindon Fiddler.

Adjacent to the school, one building in Much Hoole which has had many changes both in name and architecturally over the years was the original *"Rose and Crown Inn"*, shown here in the early 1950's. The landlady at that time and for many years previously was Mrs Ethel Ogden. Sam Brown took over for several years in the mid to late 50's and then he was followed by the most famous of its landlords, none other than Albert Pierrepoint, the most prolific English hangman of the twentieth century.

As hangman, his period of office spanned from 1932 till 1956, during which time he is reported to have executed 433 men and 17 women, quite a number of these being war criminals. One of the most notable of these was the traitor William Joyce, known throughout the war as *"Lord Haw Haw"* who strangely for a while before the war lived just up the road in Bretherton. Albert, a Yorkshire man, was the third in line of the Pierrepoint family to be chief executioner but resigned his post in 1956 over a disagreement concerning fees and expenses; this early retirement led to him taking over as landlord at the *"Rose and Crown"*, where a sign above the bar read *"No hanging around the bar"*.

As the business card informs us, this establishment was a regular calling place for coach parties from Liverpool to Blackpool or Morecambe – especially during the illuminations season. In earlier years the inn was extended to form tea rooms, but in the heyday of the coach parties was converted to a singing room, those requiring food being catered for in the wooden fish and chip shop across the road, run by Jimmy and Sally Bolton. In its latest transformation the *"Rose and Crown"* has been re-named the *"Bangla Fusion"* Indian restaurant.

Across the road – the A59 – and on the corner of Town Lane, is the *"Black Horse Hotel"* seen here on the occasion of the annual church walking day in about 1935; within the procession we see in the background the Revd. E. C. Dunne, with John Foxcroft lending assistance to the *"Banner Girls"* who are Enid Ball, Doris Taylor, Mary Fiddler, Annie Blake, Clara Chadwick and Mary Forrest. This photograph does not do justice to the extent and architecture of the *"Black Horse"*, however it does give us a good view of Ted Halliwell's grocery and newsagent's shop.

There were no newspaper boys and girls in those days so Ted and his wife did the deliveries themselves – twice daily – around the village; on Sunday mornings he would deliver by pony and trap, but only if it was dry weather, if wet he wouldn't subject either the pony or trap to those conditions – he simply got wet himself !

We have another photograph taken from the same position but at a much earlier date; notice the face lift which the *"Black Horse"* has been given in the first picture. Judging by their clothing, the two bystanders in this picture appear to be from a different era than those actually taking part in the procession.

From those early days of the 20th century we see in one photograph two aspects of the procession at that time – the banner and the morris dancers. Sadly the ravages of time and a particularly windy walking day in the early 1970's saw the end of the large banner, to be replaced with one which is much smaller. Happily the morris dancers still feature with increasingly younger members as time goes on, and the foibles of fashion have been reflected in the dancers' dresses over the years.

From the year 1937 with headmaster Richard Rymer and teachers Miss Wiggans and Miss Proctor we see L to R back row – Mary Wignall, Alice Ball, Frances Kirby, Margaret Harrison, Alice Johnson, Molly Barker and Frances Jagger; centre row – Gladys Barker, Olive Frear, Annie Taylor and Nelly Forshaw; front row – Kathleen Walmsley, Nellie Sutton, Peggy Cook, Bunty Frear, Dorothy Taylor and Joan Hignett.

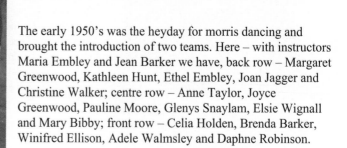

The early 1950's was the heyday for morris dancing and brought the introduction of two teams. Here – with instructors Maria Embley and Jean Barker we have, back row – Margaret Greenwood, Kathleen Hunt, Ethel Embley, Joan Jagger and Christine Walker; centre row – Anne Taylor, Joyce Greenwood, Pauline Moore, Glenys Snaylam, Elsie Wignall and Mary Bibby; front row – Celia Holden, Brenda Barker, Winifred Ellison, Adele Walmsley and Daphne Robinson.

RECTORY HOOLE

Moving down the very winding Town Lane we come to the rectory, built in 1867 by Revd. Robert Brickel, which was to be the home of six rectors and their families, until being superseded by the present one in 1993. This photograph comes from the Edmund Charles Dunne era, circa 1930.

Town Lane is known locally as *"Hoole Town"* and contains some substantial properties as well as farm houses and cottage dwellings. It was so called because at one time it was the local centre of population, being on the stagecoach route to and from the *"Black Horse"* coaching inn and the turnpike road. The lane still retains its rural atmosphere and is substantially as shown here; the only change in the last 60 years to the section shown is that the wall in the foreground has now gone and Jolly's farm directly behind has been rendered.

TOWN LANE. HOOLE.

Here we have *"Manor House Farm"* on the corner of Town Lane and Brook Lane. Whilst the ancient property is still standing this section of Brook Lane is now named with the rest of the road *"Town Lane"*. Until the beginning of the 21st century this was the home of the Martindale family and early members can be seen here with their faithful dog standing watch. Other points of interest are the stone slab fence, the very tall kitchen chimney and the milk kits awaiting collection.

From Town Lane we move into Moss House Lane and to one of the oldest and most primitive rows of cottages in the village, now however extensively modernised in the area known as 'Goose Green'. The white gabled house is detached and was built considerably later than the cottages. The one shown with the black door was lived in by the family of Thomas Chadwick from the late 19th century until the 1930's.

An anecdote remembered from times past was when a passing cow found its way through the open door into the *'parlour'* and was astonished to see its reflection in the mirror. It also caused some difficulty in its removal!

As Town Lane features *"Manor House Farm",* so here in Moss House Lane we see *"Manor Farm"*, or at least its very substantial perimeter wall and gate-posts. In the distance can be seen the old corn mill – the disused remains of which still stand alongside the row of mill cottages. From here we can choose to turn right down Carr Lane to Bretherton or take a walk over the fields via footpaths to Leyland, alternatively we can retrace our steps through the area which was the centre of Methodism in the village.

As we return towards the junction with Smithy Lane we arrive at the Hoole Methodist church and it is on record that there were Methodists in the village of Hoole in 1793. The oldest circuit books go back to 1823 when Hoole had 21 members. It is unfortunately impossible to say exactly where services were held but local Methodist history tells that in the early days William Webster (who became a local preacher) opened a granary for worship over his own house in Moss House Lane – as depicted by the drawing from a Methodist history booklet. The room was approached by a flight of wooden stairs on the outside of the building and the story goes that one Sunday the sexton of the *"opposing"* parish church cut down the stairs, thus imprisoning the worshippers. In 1826 a Sunday School was opened in a barn belonging to Richard Whittle and in 1828 both Sunday school and church services were conducted over Mr. Webster's weaving shed.

In 1848 a new brick church was built, in Moss House Lane. It is seen here with the present chapel, built in 1882, behind; the gathering would suggest that this photograph was taken on the occasion of the dedication and opening of the new chapel prior to the demolition of the old building.

This photograph shows the church in the late 1940's, prior to the removal of the front wall and railings, making way for today's more open aspect.

In the formal group we see the Hoole Wesleyan chapel choir taken in 1910. Identifiable members are, back row – centre Tommy Hewitson, right – Charlie Oates; second row – left Will Hewitson, Elizabeth Hunt and Jack Ball, right centre Mary Hindle, far right Jack Hugh Mayor and Annie Rigby; third row – from third left Cissie Rimmer, Madge Maughan, Alice Holt, Margaret Hewitson, John Rimmer and Mary Oates; front – left Matt Holt, second right Ernie Holt. Three years later in more relaxed mood, we find them setting out in a charabanc (possibly the choir trip); note the bulb horn and headlight, with spare tins of petrol underneath the vehicle, and one can only wonder what the effect was when the folding roof was erected!

On a less formal occasion in the early 1900's, we find a working party decorating and cleaning the chapel with, on the smaller photo, the object of their work – the chapel interior. Identifiable on the picture from the top row left are – Dick Holt, Will Thornley, Jack Hugh Mayor, Tommy Hewitson, John Rimmer, Alec Holt, Dick Hunt, Frank Hewitson; second row – John Hunt, Revd. Paul Bacon, Harry Hunt, Charlie Hindle; third row – Alice Hunt, Bella Mayor, Betty Webster, Maggie Hewitson, Maggie Jackson; front row – Bella Hunt, Jane Hunt, Kate Wilson, Lily Holt.

Having rounded the junction into Smithy Lane, this long view from the 1930's shows the smithy in the far distance, where the blacksmith was Robert Wilson. The property in the right foreground is the *"Old School House"* which dates from 1760. Children were taught in a room of this detached dwelling until the present school was built in 1850 by the Revd. Brickel. Whilst the property was actually a weaver's cottage it had the grand title of *"Hoole Free School"*.

Adjacent to the *"Smithy Inn"* and opposite the smithy was Holt's shop and Post Office. In the photograph, taken about 1950, we see Matt Holt and postman Jimmy Banks. The wartime advert is of John Lund's butcher's shop: together these two retail outlets were the *"centre of all knowledge"* in the village.

Leaving Smithy Lane we turn right into Liverpool Old Road where on the left is a row of semi-detached houses known as *"Spring Bank"*; the nearest of these was also a nursery with three or four greenhouses. Bill Ball, who lived there, was also the local barber, cutting his customers' hair in one of the greenhouses. The nursery has now gone and this end property has recently been extended to double its original size.

5360.   LIVERPOOL ROAD, MUCH HOOLE.

Looking right from *"Spring Bank"* we see *"Prospect House"* on the right with Brook Lane turning to the left. In the distance can be seen *"Critchley's Farm"* which, like other properties in the centre of the village, no longer operates as a working farm.

Other land in this area became the site of the village hall. In January 1947 a meeting was held to discuss the probability of such a venture. As a result, a committee, seen here, was formed. From left to right, back row – R Wignall, unknown, A E Robinson, J Burns, J Sutton, G Barker; second row – J Smith, M Holt, Mrs O Day, Mrs Penswick, T Harrison, T Pickles; third row – J Foxcroft, T Day (Secretary), T Orritt (Chairman), J Hornby (Vice Chairman), E Holt (Treasurer).

At the second meeting the starting of a fund was discussed, the name to be *"Hoole Village Hall Fund"*, banking to be with the Midland Bank and auditors Sam Bolton and Fred Gabbot being appointed. Sub-committees were formed to be in charge of proposed activities, e.g. dances, football, tennis, bowling etc., with a women's section under the presidency of Mrs Penswick.

At the third meeting, as a tribute to the fallen in the recent war, it was unanimously agreed that the name of the fund should be rescinded and the title *"Hoole Village Memorial Hall"* be accepted. Various sites for the hall were considered, the eventual one chosen being land on Liverpool Old Road belonging to Lindon Walmsley and purchased for £968, some of which could be reclaimed from grants.

In those early days many sporting and fund raising activities took place, amongst which were dances held at Worsley's Ballroom Preston, which, as an added attraction, local sporting hero Tom Finney attended. He is pictured here with some committee members at that time, from the left – Tom Pickles, Miss Elizabeth Buck, Mrs Betty Greenwood, Mrs Elizabeth Orritt, Tom Finney, Mrs Clara Chadwick, Mrs Hetty Chadwick, Jack Staziker and chairman Tommy Orritt.

Shorthorn Bull, "DUKE OF HOOLE." Photo by C. H. Parsons.

In a rural community such as Hoole, agriculture played a prominent part in the lifestyle of many of its residents. One of its most formidable residents at the beginning of the 20th century was *"Duke of Hoole"*, a prize winning shorthorn bull, bred by Richard & Thomas Harrison. In 1908 *"Duke"* won 5 championships, the Shorthorn Society's prize and 12 firsts at leading shows; in 1909 he followed this up with 3 firsts and 3 championships, including that of the Royal Agricultural Society of England. The bull was then sold for £1750 and exported to Argentina.

It is hardly surprising that with a background such as this it was to agriculture that the village turned for fundraising, and was famous for its wartime efforts in support of the Red Cross Fund. This show catalogue with supporting advertisers dates from 1944 when £1,756 was raised – surpassing the previous year's efforts by £440.

After the war those connected with the fund-raising shows channelled their efforts towards the young people and in 1949 we see a flourishing Young Farmers' Club, which met above Theo Robinson's barn in Town Lane. The land which was to become the site for the shortly-to-be-built Village Memorial Hall was also used for a Young Farmers' field day, and here we see organisers from both the Young Farmers' and Village Hall committees working together – John Sutton, second left, having borrowed the family vehicle for the occasion.

Proceeding along Liverpool Old Road one of the most splendid homes was, rather strangely, named *"Park Cottage"* which, despite almost being overgrown, can be seen to be large and grand. It was for many years the home of Mr and Mrs Charles Maughan, and is yet another property which, for a stranger, would today be difficult to recognise from these two photographs.

We now approach the old boundary between the villages of Much Hoole and Little Hoole, evidence of which still stands in the shape of the boundary stone at the end of Raikes Row. Across the road is a small burial ground and it was here that in 1854 the Primitive Methodists of Little Hoole built their own chapel. This was, as can be seen from the picture, a rather austere building where, as records show, the first musical accompaniment for services was the purchase in 1864 of a bass fiddle for £1.0s.0d. and two years later a harmonium was bought at a cost of £17.0s.0d., this in turn being replaced by a new organ purchased in 1875 for £26.11s.6d.; in the same year new carpets and mats were acquired adding much to the comfort of the worshippers.

Still on Liverpool Old Road, Little Hoole, but moving into Walmer Bridge we have a neat row of semi-detached houses known as *"Bond Terrace"*, the entrance to *"Bond Farm"* being on the immediate right. The railings in front of the houses were removed during World War II to help the war effort and for many years the centre house (with the small sign above the door) was used as the local police station.

Many years ago when cattle were shipped across to Lancashire from Ireland, they were contained in the hull of the ship by rough pens. In order to make room for the cargo on the return journey the timber used for these pens was jettisoned overboard and invariably floated to the same place; an enterprising individual – presumably by the name of Bond – salvaged this timber and built the terrace with revenue from the sale of the timber.

Opposite the terrace is the present Methodist Chapel, built in 1894, the land being generously donated by local brewery owner Thomas Wilkins. The foundation stones were laid on 23rd March 1894 by Charles Grierson – manager of the local cotton mill – two staunch church members William Webster and Catherine Stuart Cookson, and another stone in memory of the late John Webster.

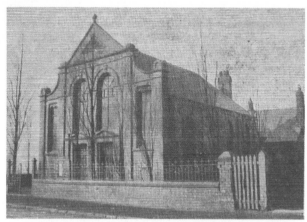

These two smaller pictures show the trustees and a group of the young ladies' Bible class from those early days.

In the area of Walmer Bridge at the end of the nineteenth century, for many who worshipped at the chapel employment would have been at Horrocks' and Crewdson's cotton mill, built in 1852, many men and women walking long distances to their work, six days a week. Boys and girls were *'half-timers'* at the age of twelve, i.e. working half a day and spending the other half day at school – being paid 2s-6d a week, the working day beginning at 6.00am. The mill closed in 1931 and during the Second World War was used by the government as a naval store. After the war the site was used for transportation businesses and has now been re-developed as a sheltered accommodation complex – *"Old Mill Court"*.

The *"Walmer Bridge Co-operative Wholesale and Provident Society Limited"* occupied a prime site at the corner of Liverpool Old Road and Gill Lane. As well as selling provisions the store had a large section selling shoes, clothing and dress materials, and also included a house (on the left of the photo) for the manager.

Competition to the '*Co-op*' came when Johnnie Walsh returned home from the First World War and converted the front room of his cottage in Mill Row into a veritable *"Alladin's cave"* of merchandise. One could hardly ask for the wrong thing and children would call on their way home from school spending their pennies on the *'sweets of the day'* on offer. He continued this business until the 1970's and also operated as a clock and watch repairer, being affectionately known as *"Johnnie Clock"*.

Other cottage businesses were the village Post Office and butcher's shop located in the front rooms of cottages adjacent to the *"Walmer Bridge Inn"*. Whilst these two cottages are now gone, the third remains as part of the now extended inn, which in the 1930's – when this photo was taken – would be selling *"Groves and Withnall"* ales. Also gone is the wooden fish and chip shop seen behind the telegraph pole.

Still in Walmer Bridge, in an early photograph showing *"Mill Row Cottages"* prior to Johnnie Walsh's days as a shopkeeper, we see the old Little Hoole school which was replaced in 1937 with a new one about 200 yards away in Dob Lane. On the opening day the scholars walked in procession from the old to the new. For many years this building remained empty, being then converted for use as a light industrial commercial enterprise *"Longton Cash Register"* and subsequently has reverted to a pre-school day nursery.

The class shown would be photographed about 1920, identifiable members (along with headmaster Mr Norbury) being: bottom row – 2nd left Ellen Mortimer, holding date board – Margaret Pickles, 2nd right Jane Carr; second row 3rd left Albert Hewitson; third row – 2nd and 3rd left Tom Harrison and Tom Pickles, far right Dick Rawcliffe.

Photographed in front of the new school, which was their base in the early 1940's, we see the local Home Guard with their leader, school headmaster Tom Griffiths. Front row left – Hugh Bamford and Tom Staziker, centre – Tom Griffiths and Jack Hunt; second row centre – Bill Holden, George Strickland and right Frank Bond; top row – 2nd left Hugh Coulton and third right Frank Webster.

24

Having visited the main parts of Hoole and Walmer Bridge we must not forget that a section still remains, having been cut off from the remainder in 1926 by the construction of the arterial road to be known as *"Liverpool New Road"*, changing the face of Hoole as it crossed the old meandering roads to become the A59.

Liverpool New Road, Hoole (Lancs)

Towards its southern end in the 1930's a row of new houses was built known locally as *"The Dales"* as each was given a name such as Grisedale, Dentdale etc. In the middle distance can be seen a large two-chimney-stacked-house *"Douglas House"* – local lore says it was once a Post Office bearing a sign above the door stating *"Licensed to sell snuff and tobacco"*.

In this vicinity a family business – originally started by his brothers in 1901 and operated from the family home adjacent to the *"Black Horse"* hotel – was being run by Jack Ball. Jack was engaged in repairing the prevailing form of transport, the bicycle, but saw the potential the new road offered and constructed first the wooden garage and a year later the house. He continued repairing bicycles and sold basic hardware from the garage. The building was used by local lads as a friendly meeting place in the evenings and school holidays; they would sit on boxes around the wood burning stove whilst drinking the *'dandelion and burdock'* which Jack sold.

These two photographs, taken around 1931, show the petrol pumps with long swinging arms, enabling the vehicles to simply pull up at the side of the road whilst being filled with petrol (no diesel in those days).

Eventually the wooden building was demolished and in due course a more modern filling station was built on adjacent land, being called *"Brooklawn Service Station"* – the photograph shows one of the proprietors, Bill Swarbrick, in 1963. After about 20 years the filling station building was again demolished and yet again slightly re-sited, but once more its life was only short lived, and following a few years of dereliction the site now holds a small development of six new houses, built in 2004, known as *"Brooklawns"*.

Another garage at this time was owned by brothers Tom and Bill Staziker. They too decided to relocate and moved from the old road to a site on the arterial road close to the Brook Lane crossing, again a house being built alongside the old wooden garage. This garage was eventually re-built and under successive ownership , notably Jack Taylor, Harry Lord and eventually Fred Kirkham, transferred from mechanical to car body repairs and is now a used car sales outlet owned by Nigel Garlick.

The photographs show two different modes of transport of the day, a motorbike and sidecar in front of the garage, with on the other Tom Staziker standing beside two customers (Laurel and Hardy look-alikes) in their open-top Singer.

Around the same time, Luke Suthers opened his garage, a small wooden building with a petrol pump, towards the southern end of the village at the junction of the Liverpool Old and New Roads – a prime site between the villages of Little Hoole and Walmer Bridge. Two facelifts later, to conform with health and safety requirements, the current brick building was opened as *"Star Garage"* (did this name come from the Wills *"Star"* cigarettes as shown on the photograph?); note also the advertisements for *"Capstan"* and *"Three Castles"* cigarettes, and it can be seen on the pump that a gallon would in those days cost *'eleven pence ha'penny'*. The workman shown is Harry, one of Luke's sons, aged about 15, who eventually became the proprietor, to be succeeded by his son Peter, the current proprietor. This photograph was reproduced in the 1980's when cousins Peter and John (son of Harry's brother Fred) were running the garage jointly.

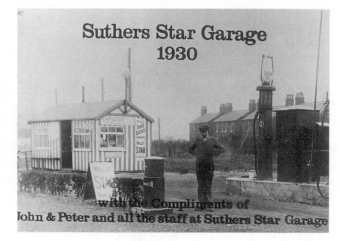

Suthers Star Garage
1930

with the Compliments of
John & Peter and all the staff at Suthers Star Garage

Station Road, Hoole (Lancs)

Copyright. HOOL. 10.

From its junction at the roundabout Station Road began life as *"Tongues Lane"*, later to become *"Marsh House Lane"*, and then with the coming of the railway and obviously the station, this upper section was re-named *"Station Road"* – the lower section remaining *"Marsh House Lane"*, and ironically it is only since the closure of the railway under Dr Beeching's axe that the whole of the road (mainly for easier identification) has been named 'Station Road'. Together with the adjoining roads of Brook Lane and Pine Avenue this small community forms the North West corner of Little Hoole. The white cottage central to the photograph, formerly the home of the Chadwick and then the Wilson families, has now been demolished.

Here we see *"Marsh House Lane"* with Lower Marsh Farm (for many years the home of the Hawthornthwaite family and now demolished) to the right, with Manor House just left of centre and Marsh House Farm further up the road in the distance. As recently as 1978 the marsh bank collapsed, flooding the area when the tide came up to the doors of these properties; this was exactly 50 years on from the previously-remembered flooding of the area, when it drowned cattle at Lower Marsh Farm and washed hay stacks away.

Viewed from two slightly different angles *"Manor House"* on Station Road is one of the finest in the area. Built in 1692, its features bear strong resemblance to *"Carr House"* and St. Michael's Church, all three being listed buildings. The link with all three does not stop there, as *"Manor House"* served as the rectory for the parish for many years until 1867, when it was replaced by a new building much nearer to the church in Town Lane. Since the 1950's it has been the home of the Burney family who, when they moved in had extensive clearing to do as it had been unoccupied for some time, was heavily overgrown and completely covered with ivy. The platform lamp in the foreground was purchased and erected following the closure of the nearby railway station in 1964.

Looking from across the road this photograph shows the extent of *"Manor House"* with the newer and slightly taller of the buildings to the left. This section of the house was originally lined with oak panelling but in 1928 when the property was sold along with many other dwellings owned by the Wilkins Brewery estate, one of the conditions of the sale was that the panelling was to be sold at an additional cost of £100 above the selling price of £450 – the buyer of the house did not pay this additional sum, the result being that the panelling was bought and removed by an American buyer.

Never one of the busiest passenger stations on the Preston to Southport line, due to its remote location from the centre of the village, Hoole Station, viewed here in the Southport direction was not without its interest and characters – in the smaller picture we see one of these characters from comparatively recent years, Ernie Snell, with the station's only permanent mode of transport, setting off to deliver a recently-received parcel.

Just off the main picture to the left was the goods siding and yard – one of the largest on the line – which was mainly used by coal merchants who had their supplies delivered there on goods wagons. The station formed a fascination for many local children and several recall being allowed to help pull the signal levers and wind the big wheel which opened and closed the crossing gates from within the signal box, the corner of which is just visible to the extreme right of the main picture.

Here we have a better view of the signal box looking in the direction of Preston with the Chadwick family eagerly awaiting the arrival of the train to take them for a day out to Southport.

The next station on the line in the Preston direction was '*Longton Bridge*' where this photograph, taken around 1960, shows a gathering of railway employees. A senior official is seen making a retirement presentation, with '*Little Ernie*' from Hoole having joined them for the occasion; the other employee on the left has also made a special trip, presumably on an official bicycle, as he has forgotten to remove his cycle clips.

In the direction of Southport the next station was '*Hesketh Bank*', being separated from Hoole by the River Douglas. The Douglas railway bridge – now demolished – formed the only direct link between the two villages, and it was common on Sunday afternoons, after Sunday School, for teenagers to walk down Haunders Lane on to Much Hoole marsh and use this crossing to the slightly busier village of Hesketh Bank. The picture of the bridge over the river shows in the background, on the opposite bank, some of the buildings of Alty's brickworks.

Here we find a small gathering on the station to wave to the group of passengers on board the last train, making its final journey to Southport on Sunday 6th September 1964, before the line was closed along with many other branch lines. Out of the picture and to the left of the small waiting room for Preston-bound passengers, were garden areas beautifully kept and well cared for by Alan Hunt who shared the duties at the station with Ernie Snell.

Participation and community spirit have always formed part of the life of the village of Hoole, which in the early 1900's had its own brass band, the bandmaster rejoicing in the name of James Dehli Pye! This photograph – taken at the western end of Longton church – includes George Barnish at second left of the back row with William Chadwick in front of him.

Some fifteen years later, on a much less formal occasion, the villagers had got together a motley crew to form a jazz band. Third from the left wearing a horizontally striped shirt is Tom Holt junior, next and central is Bob Barnish, with second right Bill Barker; kneeling to the left of the drum is Bill Rhodes and on the extreme right, looking more like a ringmaster than a conductor, is Tom Holt senior.

Sport played a big part in the social life of the village with '*sports days*' being popular. Here from one such event on Sept. 3rd 1910, is a programme which would cost you 2d, with tea provided by the Sunday School at the princely sum of 6d.

Moving on to the season of 1938/39 the Longton and Walmer Bridge football team won the Lancashire Football Association Division IIIA Championship Trophy. Identifiable members are, back row extreme left – Fred Howard with third from the right Jim Farrington next to Harry Turner; middle row second left Bill Stanley then Jack Hornby next to John Burrows. Matt Farrington is seated bottom left.

With the advent in 1940 of the Revd. Watkins, to lighten the gloom of the war the girls of the church formed a concert party with the name of *"Hoole Young Folks"*. Left to Right back row – Nellie Forshaw, Revd. Watkins, Mary Wignall, Bunty Frear, Mary Blake, Edith Frear, Betty Hewitson, Helen Chadwick; front row – Frances Kirby, Annie Frear, Mary Fiddler, Ellen Holden, Alice Ball, Annie Taylor, Olive Frear, Nellie Sutton.

At the end of hostilities they once again got together, and here we see them in 1947, with the addition of a few new members, at a celebratory concert.

At the same time, shortly after the war, the young men of the village were also grouping together, and after the toss of a coin to decide the name, the Hoole and Walmer Bridge football clubs combined under the name of *"Walmer Bridge FC"* and in 1948 – in their red and white striped shirts – won the locally much sought after *"Hesketh Medals Knockout Competition"*. They had a good incentive – it had been 24 years since a Walmer Bridge team had carried off the trophy – and committee member Jack Coulton promised them (with wives and girlfriends) a treat if they won. True to his word they all enjoyed a day in Blackpool with seats at the circus. Team members were, back row – Des Alty, John Harrison, Les Waite, Jack Staziker, Jack Chadwick, Harry Mee and Bert Dickinson. The formidable forward line was made up from the Orritt brothers with their '*adopted brother*' Lindon Fiddler. Seated from left to right they are Ronnie, Terry, Les, Lindon and Wilf.

Returning to our starting point, we look at the toll bar itself. In its day it saw many travellers, from grand coaches to farm wagons, and it was a sad day when the decision was taken to demolish it in favour of the modern roundabout. Before this took place the building was a house and a shop – a meeting place for folks from all three directions.

Maybe the bicycle leaning against the wall was that of the photographer or a customer, or could it have been left – as was the local custom – by someone wishing to travel on other transport to Preston or Southport, knowing that it would still be there on their return?

Our journey now takes us eastward to Bretherton and Croston, but before leaving our starting point we can glance at the nearby Bretherton windmill which served the local farms and community. The mill on this site was, from the 1700's worked by generations of the Chadwick family, until the death of Thomas Chadwick in 1893 – he, incidentally married Elizabeth Taylor who lived at *"Carr House"*. The mill – as is seen in the first picture – became derelict, then in the 1950's was converted – as the second picture shows – into a house.

Standing just behind the site of the toll bar is *"Carr House"* – the most famous property in Bretherton and the vicinity. Built in 1613 of hand-made Dutch brick, the inscription over the doorway tells us that Thomas Stones of London and Andrew Stones of Amsterdam built the house for their brother John, a farmer. Both of John's brothers were '*in trade*', Andrew dealing in woollen cloth to Amsterdam with Thomas operating various importation enterprises from Spanish grain, French hops and Virginian tobacco – sometimes falling foul of excise officers. On the return voyages from Amsterdam the hull of the ship was filled with ballast – in the form of Dutch bricks, and it was these bricks which were used to construct Carr House, Manor House and Hoole Church.

In 1638 Andrew purchased the Manor of Hoole, with its buildings and lands, and moved into Carr House (John having left to live in Eccleston) and was in residence in 1639 when the gifted young astronomer Jeremiah Horrocks lived within the household, being most likely a tutor to the children. Whilst also carrying out his clerical duties at Hoole Church, Horrocks calculated and observed the first recorded *"Transit of Venus"* across the face of the sun – an event which was to become of international importance in astronomical circles.

The photograph clearly shows a connecting line from the top to the bottom windows, being a channel cut into the brickwork and would have qualified the two windows to be counted as one, thereby evading more excessive '*window tax*'. Since those eventful days the house has seen many owners and occupants; whilst they were mostly farmers it did in the 1980's house a *"Dolls' Museum"*, but is now a well-restored private residence.

As we travel further into Bretherton we approach the War Memorial, originally erected in memory of local men who gave their lives in WWI, being unveiled by Miss Clare of Bank Hall. A local lady, Sarah Bamford, whose brother served in that war wrote a poem to mark the unveiling, the first verse of which reads:-

Just a simple granite cross
In memory of those who are gone,
A token of love and deepest respect
For the lads who will never come home.

The signpost as seen in the photograph gives priority to the roads to the right but in earlier days Eyes Lane, to the left, would have been well used, leading as it does to the carriage drive of *'Bank Hall'* – the home at that time of Sir Harcourt Clare, Clerk of the Lancashire County Council, and his much loved and respected family.

The Banastre family appear to have been the earliest occupants of *"Bank Hall"*, which was constructed in the early 18th century and extensively re-modelled in 1832/33. Progressing through their heirs with various names through marriage, it eventually passed to the Powys family (the Lilford baronetcy). At the present time it is in a sad state of dereliction and is the subject of appeal by an action group for its restoration.

In its time the hall has been host to many celebrations, including the arrival of the Hon. John Powys and his wife in June 1895, and on the occasion in 1913 when King George V and Queen Mary passed through on their way from Preston to Southport, when the school children lined the road – the little girls with red hoods and the boys wearing red sashes provided by Mrs Clare, who received a message from the Queen when their car stopped near the gate.

From the war memorial we enter South Road where, viewed from the junction with Pompian Brow, we see in the foreground of these buildings, the old Wesleyan Chapel. Until the 1970's Bretherton sustained three places of worship. The Wesleyan Chapel was the smallest in size and in following. For many years it was thought that Methodism would not survive alongside the stronger Congregational and Anglican followings of the village. Sure enough so it was that this building ceased to be used for worship in the mid 1980's and during 1988/9 was converted into a private house. The organ was donated to the Bishop Rawsthorne School in Croston, and whilst the interior was converted into separate rooms the appearance of the exterior remains largely unchanged.

Looking at the cluster of buildings from the opposite direction (this photograph being taken from in front of the railings and entrance to the Congregational Church), in the foreground we have a pair of semi-detached dwellings, but central in both pictures is the baker's shop with bakery behind. Until the 1960's this was one of the many shops that Bretherton was able to sustain. However, one by one, these small businesses closed down, and whilst it has had a somewhat rocky passage, this establishment thankfully still remains.

If the columns and façade of the Congregational Church were not enough to tell us that this is a Victorian building, then the date of 1896 on the canopy confirms this fact, and it was on the 1st of June in that year when this church was opened. This, however, was not the first building, the original having been built in 1819, some 33 years after the Congregational movement came to Bretherton when, in 1786, Revd. William Roby of Manchester preached the first sermon here as he took up a teaching post in the local free school. Later in life he was to become a distinguished minister of the Independents, a founder member of both the *London Missionary Society*" and the *"British & Foreign Bible Society"*.

Bretherton.

Come and help us in our task
On this happy day,
Now's the opportunity,
Grasp it while you may.
Reaching out a helping hand —
Each may do their part,
Giving with a cheerful smile
And a cheerful heart.
This is what we all may do
In this world of ours,
Only let us give our best—
Nothing but the flowers.
And our lives will happy be,
Lord if we but follow thee.

Churches need our best support
Help them while you may;
Useless let us not stand by,
Render aid to-day.
Constant in your little task,
Happy from the first to last.

Bless, O Lord, this Church of thine
And this effort too,
Zealous workers, with God's help
Always peace and plenty crown ;
And when our last task we've given
Rest, sweet rest, in heaven.

As this acrostic suggests – again written by Sarah Bamford, in support of the bazaar to be held on Thursday 4th and Saturday 6th of December 1924 – this place of worship has had a strong following since those early days. At the time when most Congregational churches amalgamated with those of the Presbyterian following, to form the *"United Reformed Church"*, the Ebenezer Congregational Church at Bretherton elected to remain independent, and still remains so.

In this photograph we see in the foreground *"Chapel House"* which over the years has been the home of many chapel stalwarts and their families. Central to the picture is the Sunday School which adjoins the chapel and was to house the overspill congregation in September 1969, when the radio programme *"Sunday Half Hour"* was broadcast from here and was the highlight of the celebrations commemorating the 150th anniversary of the original chapel.

The main body of the church was filled with a large choir augmented from various churches in Bretherton, Croston, Eccleston, Hoole, Longton, Tarleton, Hesketh Bank, Leyland and Penwortham, the proceedings being announced by broadcaster Keith Macklin.

Some twenty one years after its Congregational neighbour, the parish church of Bretherton was constructed and in 1840 was consecrated and dedicated to St. John the Baptist, the area having until then, as with other *'townships and hamlets'* in the vicinity, been situated within the parish of Croston. Since the 1960's the size of the parish of Bretherton has meant that its church could not sustain a full time priest and in the main during that time its incumbents have been appointed with the additional role of teacher at the *"Bishop Rawsthorne School"* in Croston; others have been involved with diocesan duties – the most notable of these being the appointment of Bishop Donald Nestor (one of the Diocesan Auxiliary Bishops) as parish priest from 1992 until 2000. Since then history has reversed and now it is once more under the wing of St Michael and All Angels at Croston.

Inevitably many alterations and improvements have been made to the church since its erection, a quotation from a local newspaper in October 1916 reading – *"Bretherton News: At present we are engaged, much against our will, in taking down the spire of the church, which has been in a dangerous condition for some time past. We had no idea it was so out of plumb."*

Sarah Bamford (the *'Bretherton Bard'*) was moved to put pen to paper describing the tranquillity of the village in the early 1900's and across the road from the church, along with Church Farm, stand many interesting farmhouses now converted and modernised into well kept residences.

One such is *"Holly Farm"* where, until the late 1970's, generations of the appropriately named Bretherton family lived. The last of this family to live at Holly Farm was Elizabeth (Lizzie) a hard working, Christian lady of great character with a ready wit. One of nine children, she is pictured here in about 1912 with her youngest brother, Norrie. Note the water pump, which was an essential piece of equipment on all of the farms in those days of no piped water supply.

Adjacent to Holly Farm is *"Rose Farm"* and in this picture from the late 1800's we see the Wilsons, John and Margaret with their daughters Kitty and Lizzie.

Adjacent to the parish church is the village school, but between the two lie the rectory (no longer used as such since Bretherton ceased to be an independent parish), and two cottages which were the original school and teacher's home. The inscription over the porch door of the old school reads . . .

THIS FREE SCHOOL WAS ERECTED AND BUILT AT THE PROPER COSTS: AND CHARGES OF JAMES FLETCHER OF LONDON MARCHANT : AND AT THE BEQUEST OF MISTRIS JANE FLETCHER HIS WIFE WHO WAS BORNE IN THIS TOWNE :JUNE THE FOURTEENTH ANNODONI 1653

The Charity Commissioners' return for the Parish of Croston in 1898 includes the *"Township of Bretherton"*. Referring to the school, it states *"An old book relating to this school contains a statement entitled 'A true description or Narrative of the first Rising or beginning of the School of Bretherton' "*.

 In substance it stated that Jane, the wife of James Fletcher, who was born at Bretherton, had been requested by John Cliffe of Bretherton to give something towards the setting up of a school there. After her death her husband informed John Cliffe that monies had been left in her will for this purpose and that he was willing to carry out her wishes providing the inhabitants of Bretherton would contribute; following initial reluctance on the part of some people, final arrangements were made in 1653 for the erection of a school, under the administration of feoffees (trustees) *". . . . . intending the continuance and maintenance of the said building to be a free school for the teaching of the youth and children of the inhabitants of the town of Bretherton . . . . ."*.

Subsequently, around 1848, a small portion of charity-owned land was taken by the East Lancashire Railway for the purpose of constructing their line from Preston to Liverpool. The price of the land was fixed by valuers appointed by the trustees and the company, and with the addition of grants sufficient monies were obtained for the erection of this – '*the new school*', for boys and girls, the old one being converted into a residence for the school mistress. This photograph was taken in the 1960's.

Excerpts from an 1898 report on the *". . . . Narrative of the first Rising or Beginning of the School of Bretherton"* state that *"an annual meeting of the feoffees should be held on 10ᵗʰ April, either at Bretherton or Ormskirk. . . . that a register should be kept for the public good of the school and put into the hands of some honest person . . . any scholar behaving disorderly and wickedly, upon due proof had against him, on complaint of the schoolmaster, should by any six of the feoffees be expelled out of the school and not admitted again until satisfaction should be made by the parents of such child".*

Here in this earlier picture of the school we see in the foreground the wooden cabin which was the village *"clogger's shop"*, taken over and operated in the 1920's by *"Billy"* Ashton who came from Leyland.

Farming has long been central to the lives of Bretherton folk and, like South Road, so too the parallel North Road had its share of farms, some of which are still working. Here we see a typical one in North Road, Brook Farm – the home of the Monk family. In this photograph from about 1900 we see Mrs Monk holding baby Maria, with husband Jack looking on.

Different views have been expressed as to the origins of local place names and nearby there is a row of cottages called *"Canal Leach"* (known locally as *"Cannalaitch"*): leaching is the removal of a substance by a percolating liquid, i.e. natural land drainage, and it is here that the Carr Brook channel passes Brook Farm, Brook Cottages and eventually Bretherton windmill to join the River Douglas, which separates the villages of Bretherton and Tarleton.

With a farming background such as this it is hardly surprising that Harvest Festival was an important time for all, as seen by this interior photograph of the Congregational church at harvest time, showing the minister, Mr. Meredith, in the pulpit, with Charlie Thompson, the gardener at *'Bank Hall'*, who was proud to decorate the front of the chapel, no doubt growing splendid blooms for the occasion.

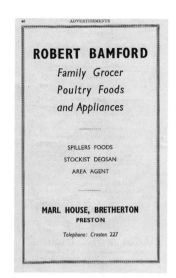

Returning to South Road at its junction with Marl Cop, and still with the farming community in mind, a possible suggestion for the origin of its name is that the land thereabouts was composed of *'marl'* (clay minerals and salt – used as fertiliser), a hill or *'bank'* being known as a *'cop'*. Here we find the corn mill and shop owned by Robert Bamford, and whilst the business still continues in nearby Midge Hall this building has been converted into an antiques shop and tea room.

The distant semi-detached houses in the other picture are seen here, as is the gate entrance to Bretherton cricket ground (not in use at the time of the photograph) which, judging by the snow covered mound, shows a wintertime scene when the football field on the opposite side of the road would be in use.
Bretherton Cricket Club was formed in 1909, joined the Southport and District League in 1925 and moved to this site in 1948.

Before leaving Bretherton and nearing its boundary with Croston there are two more properties of note. The first, set back from South Road and pictured is *"Over Hall"*. One suggestion as to the derivation of the name *"Over Hall"* is that such a property should have an overall view and be so situated as to be a good *'look out post'* for its own township or village, the upper arched window being ideal in this particular case. This photograph from the turn of the century shows Mrs Mary Bamford, whose son George subsequently married Sarah Jackson, who, after moving into Over Hall wrote her many poems – several of which are featured in this book. The other property – not shown – is *"Highfield House"*, which for a short time in the 1930's was the home of William Joyce (*"Lord Haw Haw"*).

The River Lostock forms the boundary with Croston and here this low lying area – once a clay pit, then waste land – is now known as *"Twin Lakes Fisheries"*, a nature reserve and haven for anglers. During the time between the two great wars another link was formed between the two villages when large buckets carrying the clay from this site in Bretherton were conveyed on an overhead system to the Crompton brickworks in Croston, down *"Brick Kiln Lane"* which ran alongside the Preston to Liverpool railway line.

As we leave Bretherton behind we cross the railway line, into the ancient village of Croston. Forking right into Station Road, today we thread our way through lines of motor vehicles both stationary and moving – a far cry from the days of our photographs when popular church processions marched unhindered along the road, invariably accompanied by a brass band and always including three decorated lorries similar to the one pictured here. Farmers were proud when their carts were used for the procession and gave them a good scrubbing up for the occasion, the decorating of the floats taking place on the previous evening in their barns or outbuildings.

These annual processions were popular in all of the villages of this area , in some cases being a joint ecumenical event, in others organised by individual churches, they could be named *"Tea Party Day"*, *"Walking Day"*, *"Field Day"*, the *"Annual Walk of Witness"*, but Croston was – and has still remained unique – in naming its particular event *"Coffee Day"*. A real day of celebration when the procession made its way through the village, via Croston Hall, where they were greeted by Squire de Trafford who served coffee and refreshment to the walkers.

Two typical scenes from the days of cobbled streets. The first – taken from where now is Lonsdale Drive, by local photographer Wm. Spencer – shows a section of those taking part walking into the village along Station Road, the other entering the opposite end of Station Road from Town Road at the junction with Westhead Road. As well as featuring the brass band, this photograph shows the old police station and an advertising board urging us to eat more fruit.

One occasion of great rejoicing took place in January 1856 when John Cottam, a soldier and a native of Croston, arrived at the railway station, was immediately transferred to a carriage and drawn through the town preceded by a band to the firing of guns and the ringing of church bells. Aged 19, the hero had been shot through the head in the siege of Sebastopol.

Station Road with large advertising boards urging the people of Croston to *"Vote for Balcarres"*. This was taken on Wednesday November 4th 1903, the day of the General Election. We see a group of supporters (including the Rector, Revd A.G.Rawstorne – later to become the Suffragan Bishop of Whalley) outside the Conservative committee rooms, with presumably the Earl of Balcarres in his handsome horse-drawn carriage.

Again in Station Road (not Town Road – as the photographer has mistakenly named it) and pictured on a sunny day – the shadows clearly seen casting across the cobbled street – we see the Methodist school. Originally built as a Sunday school, but later becoming a Methodist day school, it was eventually taken over by the Lancashire County Council in 1945. At the far end of this road it is joined by Westhead Road where, on Good Friday 1875, the foundation stone was laid for the building of a new chapel by the members of the United Methodist Free Church, who had for some years held services in an adapted pair of cottages. The church, made of Croston brick, was eventually opened in November 1881.

It is more than likely that this is the area referred to in a newspaper report stating that gas was burned for the first time in Croston, in September 1862, by two of the principal innkeepers and *"a large number of country people came to see the first illumination"*.

Now you see it – now you don't! It is, or was, the *"Horseshoe Inn"*, and with the parish church in the background stood on Town Road (the continuation of Station Road) with the smithy nearby. Standing directly opposite the '*Grapes Hotel*' it overlooked the River Yarrow , its banks washing against the rear of the building, which was demolished in the 1930's for road widening and improvements.

Viewed from the Southern end of the road, its sign has already been removed and it is looking very sad awaiting demolition. Sadness was not confined to the buildings of the area; the Yarrow was prone to flooding and a newspaper report in early 1850 tells of the death by drowning of two year old Jennet Highfield of Croston who, unknown to her mother, fell down the steps into a neighbour's flooded cellar.

The tower of the parish church can clearly be seen amid the terraced cottages, and its approach – Church Street – with its ancient stone cross and village pump forms a nostalgic picture with the cobbler's shop – the oldest building in Croston - on the left. On the busier picture, behind the man using the pump, is the smithy. This property has now been converted into a dwelling house, presently occupied by the grand-daughter of the blacksmith pictured.

Within the precincts of the churchyard stood the schoolhouse. In the 1898 Charity Commissioners' Report on the charities of the parish of Croston in 1826 it is stated that *" the Revd. James Hiet, Rector of Croston, by his will bearing the date 18th March 1662, had procured a free schoolhouse to be built in Croston churchyard, at his own great cost and trouble . . . . for the good education of the children of the said parish . . . ."*

The school was erected in 1660 and Mr Hiet ordered that each scholar should pay one shilling at entrance (six pence if the parents were poor cottagers), that the master should teach the principles of the Christian religion and that he should be allowed to receive 10 scholars for quarterly wages but this should not hinder the teaching of the free scholars.

A further item from the return states *"It appears from an entry in 1804 that a sum of £50 arising from the sale of a seat in the church . . . . should be lent to the trustees of this school to be laid out in erecting seats in the south aisle . . . . The erection of seven seats . . . . amounted to £21. 5s. 8d. of the above £50 and the residue was eventually placed in the hands of the Revd. Streynsham Master, who had been elected a trustee and had become Rector of Croston about 1799 . . . ."* The Rector does not appear to have been a very good trustee, as in 1820 he *"left England, in consequence of the embarrassed state of his pecuniary affairs which were placed in the hands of the trustees . . . .other instances will be hereinafter mentioned in which sums belonging to charities were in Mr Master's hands at the time of his leaving England"*.

Two general views show first the south elevation of the church and secondly *"Croston Rectory",* which whilst of a splendid Georgian style displays a significant amount of Dutch influence.

This wintertime view of the rectory tells its own story, and shows the *'ha-ha'* – sunken land with a small wall which, whilst keeping cattle from the rectory precinct, gave the occupants an uninterrupted rural view. In the picture of Croston ruins, the gatehouse to the rectory, with Grape Lane in the distance, also features the fingerpost pointing to Highfield Road and the next chapter of our story.

Town Road to the left leads to Highfield Road. This picture shows *'Beech House'*, the house and surgery of Dr. Duckworth who is just leaving on his rounds, chauffeured in his motor car, registered number CK.1. We also see a horse drawn carriage, giving a perfect illustration of the changing modes of travel in the first decade of the twentieth century.

Turning the corner further down the road we arrive at a neat row of cottages known as *'Cock Robin'* – which is actually a double row of cottages the second row set back from the road and running parallel to the ones shown. On the right can be seen the wall of the lodge to Croston Hall. It was no doubt along this road the carriage of the newly-wed Mr. S.C. de Trafford and his bride passed, in December 1879, having arrived by train to a resounding welcome by the villagers, their carriage being towed by nearly 50 men and women with Tarleton Brass Band playing. Mrs. De Trafford was presented with a silver bread basket by members of the Croston Hall estate.

Moving south, away from the village centre towards the village of Mawdesley and capturing the essentially rural atmosphere, Grape Lane offers the opportunity to take a look at some of the oldest and most interesting properties in Croston. The dark looking cottage in the centre of the picture is a detached residence, now painted white, and aptly named *"Vine Cottage"*.

Viewed in the opposite direction and taken from the commencement of the bend in the road on the first picture is this interesting collection of cottages, the centre one of the row of three named *"Grape Cottage"*. The thatched roof has since been replaced by slates, the upper windows protruding into the modified roof design; this apart, very little else has changed – the large stone gate post in the foreground remaining and marking the entry to a public footpath. This area in Victorian times would be largely populated by the families of workers on the Hall estate, some of whom can be seen taking a stroll.

Whilst accessible from Grape Lane, to envisage a grand entry down the Carriage Drive to Croston Hall we must return to Highfield Road, where the lodge remains to this day, standing firm as a reminder of days gone by.

As the carriage drive crosses Grape Lane we see its continuation and entrance to the hall in all its splendour in the distance. The upper section was re-built following its destruction by fire in the 1930's.

Croston Hall.

This aerial view, taken about 1959, gives an excellent picture of the hall and surrounds. The buildings on the left were the kitchen area, also used in connection with the gardens. There was also a coach-house with adjoining tack rooms, and these buildings were used during World War II by the army, many years later still bearing signs such as 'QM Stores'. Before the war necessitated all available land being used for growing food crops, the land at the rear of the hall was a fine lawn which was cut by horse-drawn mowers. The horses wore large leather shoes over their hooves to prevent them treading too heavily into the surface.

The hall stands proudly at its western elevation, whilst the interior picture shows the opulence of the grand entrance hall. Its architect was A. W. N. Pugin, who was one of the architects of the Palace of Westminster.

Quite separate from the hall, but within the grounds, stands the private family chapel, dedicated to the Holy Cross, now used by the villagers as their Roman Catholic Church, with an entrance in Grape Lane.

Whilst the chapel remains, the hall was demolished after being bequeathed to the R.C. Diocese of Liverpool on the death of the last occupant, Miss Ermyntrude de Trafford in 1964. A homely note is that Miss Ermyntrude bred and showed rabbits, winning many prizes.

A common sight until the advent of the combined harvester was the thresher, and on threshing day it was '*all hands to the pump*' .Dust and rats were in abundance as the machine noisily separated the corn into sacks, and also dispensed the chaff and the straw. Here at '*Baker's Farm*' on the banks of the Yarrow we see the steam engine being prepared to power the thresher into action on such a day.

From his Town Road shop, a much more solitary occupation was that of the food delivery man (Mr. Bannister or Mr. Ascroft?), his only companion on his daily rounds being his patient horse.

In contrast we have a line of workers from James Rigbye's Joiner's and Wheelwright's shop on Station Road, where it is obvious that the photographer has instructed that '*tools of the trade*' are to be held. From left to right we have the blacksmith with his lump hammer, three carpenter/joiners the first with a trying plane (no machines to do the job in those days), left handed rip saw and right handed tenon saw users, with possibly the most interesting along the line being the next man – a wheelwright, holding an adze, originally a shipwright's tool but very useful for shaping curved timbers. The remaining two workers hold jack planes, and not to be outdone a passing cyclist crept in on the end. Note how the timbers were stored in those days to keep them drier – with the shafts of the many carts following suit.

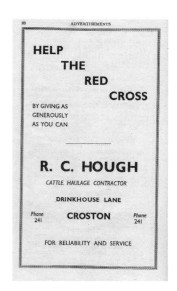
In days gone by this footbridge provided private access from the church over the River Yarrow to *"Yarrow Cottage"*.   Since its demolition in the 1950's the access across the river is by *"Town Bridge"* – opposite the Grapes Inn – alongside an area known as '*the Hillocks',* past Baker's Farm to a small self-contained community known as *"Drinkhouse"* or, as the poster from 1944 reminds us, '*Drinkhouse Lane'.*

Whilst this property remains, neither it nor any other in this area operates as a drinkhouse; the area comprises a few farm-houses and immaculately kept cottages and gardens, offering yet another unique opportunity to slip into times past in this quiet corner of Croston, separated as it is from the main part of the village by the River Yarrow.

Leaving this area via Shevington Causeway we can either turn right and back into the village along Westhead Road, or turn left into Meadow Lane and on to the village of Rufford – but that's another story!

Retracing our steps through the village and over the railway line we can vary our route through Bretherton by turning left at Highfield House into Back Lane and eventually to Eyes Lane and the war memorial. From here we once again arrive at the *"Toll Bar"*, where we begin the third stage of our *'traipse'*. Turning left we pass through an area once known as *"Bank"* – hence *"Bank Mill"*, *"Bank Hall"* and *"Bank Bridge"*, with its three arches over the dividing line of the River Douglas (at one time known as the *'Asland'*) and the Rufford branch of the Leeds & Liverpool canal.

Extract from Baines' *"History of Lancashire – Leyland Hundred"*
 "Tarleton was one of the last parishes separated from Croston . . . . . bounded on the north by Hesketh-cum-Becconsall, on the west by North Meols, on the south by Rufford, and on the east by Croston, being separated from the latter parish by the Douglas (rendered navigable in A.D. 1727). . . . ."

On the outskirts of the village the first building of note is Tarleton Old Church – the photograph being taken from the south. The crofters' cottages and farm buildings in the background are long since gone – except for a pig sty still in evidence at the first of four semi-detached houses in Coe Lane which replaced the cottages as the road was widened. The hay field in the foreground is now used as the local burial ground. According to Baines' *"History of Lancashire"* the church was erected by the Fleetwoods of Bank Hall and consecrated on the 24th July 1719, being dedicated to St. John. Further re-dedication must have taken place as locally it is known as *"St. Mary's"*. It is worth noting that the finials at the corners and apex of the roof (possibly easier to see on the right hand picture) are to the same style as those on St. Michael's Church, Hoole.

Cross Roads, Wingate, Tarleton.

Continuing uphill we arrive at Windgate corner – pronounced locally as *"Wanget"*, looking in the direction of Southport; here, in the 1930's, at this rather bleak looking junction we can see Church Road to the right (which leads to the village). Also in evidence is the R.A.C. patrol officer: later, just out of the photograph to the left – in the direction of Liverpool – an R.A.C. emergency call box was erected.

Looking towards Liverpool (now the A59), the farm buildings in the immediate foreground, flanked by the telegraph poles, are now gone. However the original *'Ram's Head Hotel'* to the right of the poles still stands with only this frontage recognisable, several phases of *'modernisation'* having completely changed the remainder. This busy junction was always a favourite spot for roadside advertising.

Liverpool Road, Tarleton.

In common with many public houses, the *"Ram's Head"* was also a working farm and Gerry Blakemore, the licensee, also provided milk for children at local schools circa 1930; here we see the dairy maid with an early delivery vehicle.

We are now proceeding northwards into Church Road. An interesting extract from an 1898 Return to the House of Commons (following a Charity Commissioners' Inquiry in 1826) refers to Tarleton School, apparently built at the corner of Blackgate Lane in 1706, with stone from an old chapel (which formerly stood on nearby land) being used for its eventual enlargement.

Various bequests and charities were given for the erection and maintenance of the building, with provision for living accommodation for the headmaster, who was appointed by a board of trustees of local men. These trustees were also responsible for selecting the 20 poor children for education, and administering the proceeds of the charities. One item states that one of six endowments is *"The old school building and site, containing 13 perches, let as a drapery and furniture store to Joseph Webster at a yearly rent of £5."*
The gross income from the six endowments was £49.

Whilst there is no photographic evidence of that original school, a barn converted into two dwellings now occupies the site, with two modern properties having replaced the abattoir which stood alongside. Adjacent is *"Horseshoe Farm"*, originally forming part of the *"Bank Hall Estate"*; now tastefully modernised, this cottage dates back to the times when warmth from the animals (also housed within) was relied upon to provide some of the heating. During the 1940's and 50's a room of this house was used as a surgery for visiting doctors on their days of call.

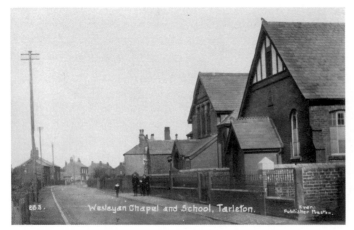

Wesleyan Chapel and School, Tarleton.

Standing across the road is the Wesleyan Chapel built in 1896, a local newspaper reporting on 29th August 1896 that *"The opening services were continued on Sunday, the pulpit being occupied by Mr John Dandy of Bootle, who preached both afternoon and evening to good congregations. The Hoole Wesleyan choir, along with their string band efficiently led the singing".*

The parish church, dedicated to the Holy Trinity, is a little further along the road. January 1889 saw the introduction of a monthly parish magazine (priced at 1d per copy) and in his New Year's address, the Revd. R.C. Fletcher – later to become Archdeacon Fletcher – referred to the fact that 1888 had been notable for the consecration of the new parish church on the 7th June. In the February edition the main item was the *"Dedication and Opening"* of the new organ, presented by Miss Marion Kennedy. A further interesting item showed that the cost of the pulpit of the new church was £60; towards this sum the churchwardens' subscription list raised £6, the remainder being collected by the exertions of Miss M.G. Rawcliffe and *"this shows what a little girl of 10 years can do when she makes up her mind to try!"*

In August 1919 the church and village celebrated the ending of WWI with a Peace Parade and it is interesting to note that whilst the first picture shows the new church with a steeple, the banner on the second one depicts it 'steepleless' – having originally been so constructed – the steeple being added later as funds would allow.

The decorated horse and lorry were obviously photographed before leaving the farm to join the procession, and for many people this area, which is a small cul-de-sac near the church, will bring back happy memories of "*Tarleton Cinema*" housed in the barn just showing on the right. For many years until the late 1950's this was the height of entertainment for Tarleton and district, with admission at 6d and double seats at the back for courting couples! The final Peace Parade photograph moves away from the centre of the village down Blackgate Lane; the white building on the right was a cobbler's shop, the large house in the centre helping to pinpoint the actual location on the south side of the road.

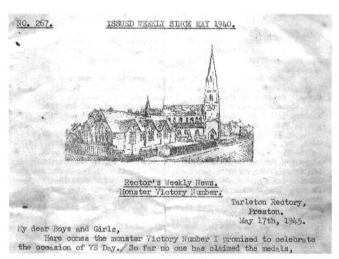

Whilst telling of peacetime celebrations, reference must be made to a unique service rendered by the local rector to the lads and lasses who took part in WWII, (not just confined to Tarleton but all the villages featured in this book). As can be seen from the picture, the weekly newsletter was first issued in 1940 and was a means of keeping the recipients in touch with home and each other.

This '*Victory Number*' ran to 15 pages and in his editorial the Revd. L.N. Forse says *"Well!!! You have done the trick properly this time, and we are all proud of you. It has been no easy walk over, but you have stuck it well and pulled it off in no uncertain manner. Tarleton takes its hat off to you and says 'Thank you, lads'"*. The letter continues and concludes *"With the thanks of all in Tarleton, and with my own prayers, and pride in you all, ever your old friend and Rector, L.N. FORSE"*

Central to village life are the church, school and the pub. In both pictures we see the church with the pub
"The Cock and Bottle" in the foreground – the school, obscured from this angle, stands between the two.
There has obviously been a passage of time between these two photographs during which the *"Cock"* – as it is locally known
– has been given a face lift, and looks not a lot different from its present appearance. In the older view the end of the
blacksmith's shop can just be seen with the carts standing outside whilst inside the horses would be being re-shod, and
together with the bicycles, pram and children this scene captures village life at the turn of the 19th to 20th century.

It was at the Cock and Bottle that a property sale was held on 20th October 1886. Notice was
given of the *"Sale by Auction of 300 acres of land, with numerous farmhouses and cottages, and
including the 'Cock and Bottle Inn', belonging to Sir Thomas George Fermor Hesketh, Bart.; in
order to give the Residents in the neighbourhood the opportunity of becoming owners of freeholds
upon easy terms of interest."* Information given showed a good rate of interest and the obligation
of the Leeds & Liverpool Canal Company to deliver manure free of toll for farming purposes.
Typical lots quoted are:-
*"Lot 1, The House – now the Post Office – and the shop in Tarleton village, with garden, occupied
by Ann Wignall, containing 1 rood, 13 perches.
Lot 10, the 'Cock and Bottle' Inn, occupied by Daniel Barron, with barn, stable, orchard and
garden, covering 1 acre, 19 perches.
Lot 17, Meadow Land between Coe Lane and the canal, delineated on the plan and called 'Jack
Crofts', occupied by Robert Topping and James Banister and containing 6 acres, 2 roods, 1
perch".*

Turning left into Gorse Lane and to the junction with Carr Lane, we see Bannistre Farm (now central to a recent development known as '*Bannistre Court'*) with chauffeur-driven cars at the start of their journey to a wedding. These luxury limousines help us to reflect on the differing types of transport used by farmers and carters for a variety of loads – the cart possibly laden with *"night soil"*. The Parkinson family were the original hauliers in Tarleton.

Returning to Church Road, the next turning to the left is Hesketh Lane but ahead is the cobbled road of *"Plox Brow"* leading to the canal, this surface being essential for the horses to keep their footing as they went downhill. The road leads directly to *"Town End Bridge"* – a swing bridge centre right on the second picture. Centre left is John Whittle's coal yard where coal was originally brought from Wigan by barges (some of which can be seen). In the background the mill still exists, although the coming of gas rendered the chimney redundant and it was taken down in two stages during the 1980's.

Returning to the Hesketh Lane junction the building in the foreground is the present site of shops – once the Co-op store; the taller barn building to the right, slightly modified, still remains.

On the left down Hesketh Lane stood this cottage, the site however having seen several changes. For most of the second half of the 20th century a small building – the office of George Mawdesley (hay straw and provision merchant) – stood here; now a much larger jeweller's shop occupies the site.

We soon arrive at the original post office which, at the time of the photograph – the 1930's – was occupied by John Pickup who also sold grocery and provisions. His daughter became Mrs Tatham and she continued the business for many years – her daughter, Miss Tatham, following her. For a long time theirs was the only telephone in the village and was the only form of instant communication for traders in the area for the sending and receiving of orders. The final picture shows the premises as the background to the renowned 'Hesketh Bank Silver Band'.

Looking back at the border between Tarleton and Hesketh Bank, along Hesketh Lane, the striped building in the centre of the picture has long since been replaced by modern shops and the present Post Office. The distinctive premises on the left are still in use as a retail outlet by Henry Alty's *"horticultural supplies and builders' merchants"*, having developed from a brickworks company which used the adjacent railway extensively. Alongside we see an early form of their transport, laden with bricks. In the foreground of the main picture the railings on both sides of the road mark the Southport to Preston railway line – now an area of housing, since becoming a victim of Dr. Beeching's axe. It was just off the photograph on the left that stood Norman McLeod's butcher's shop.

The thoroughfare now becomes *"Station Road"* although the stretch on this picture showing the Becconsall Hotel has also been referred to as *"Broadway"* (presumably being so named prior to the days of the railway). The *"Beck"* as it is locally known was originally built with three storeys, the upper floor not being replaced when the hotel was rebuilt after a devastating fire on December 10th 1931; preserved cuttings from the *"Ormskirk Advertiser"* giving a full report on this blaze are posted in the hotel for all to see. It was here, on the 21st October 1890, that a *"Formal Investigation"* was held into the *"Explosion of a Boiler at Hesketh Bank Corn Mill"*. No-one was injured but George Harrison (owner of the boiler) and John Butterworth (from whom it was purchased the year before the explosion) were each fined £25, the boiler not having been properly examined and maintained by them before and after purchase. It would appear that the explosion removed all traces of the mill, although it is known that an old windmill used to stand on Mill Lane – the grindstones still being there – on the border of Hesketh Bank with Tarleton.

STATION ROAD, HESKETH BANK

Still on Station Road and in the heart of the village, the road to the left is Newarth Lane. The properties in the foreground – once the site of the *'Bay Horse'* public house - are long since gone, being latterly the site of the Police Station, now a private dwelling. The road to the right is Becconsall Lane. This junction is perhaps an appropriate point at which to consider extracts from Baines' *"History of Lancashire – Leyland Hundred"* circa 1834. *"Hesketh is the most westerly of the five parishes which have been separated from Croston. On the north it is washed by the Ribble and on the east by the Douglas, or Asland . . .At flood-tide the Ribble is here three miles wide from Hesketh Bank to the Guide's House on Freckleton Marsh, though at low water the river is fordable under the conduct of a guide appointed for the purpose . . . Anciently a beacon was placed near the confluence of the Douglas with the Ribble, and the name 'Beacon's Hill' or 'Becconsall' is supposed to be derived from this harbinger of approaching danger . . . The parish church . . . is generally called Becconsall Chapel . . . The date of the original erection is the 16th century, and it was then used as a domestic chapel for the Becconsall family. In the year 1765 the chapel was rebuilt and enlarged. In 1821 an Act of Parliament was passed, severing Hesketh and Becconsall chapel from Croston, and elevating Hesketh to the rank of an independent parish church".* We now proceed to the second, distant, signpost which leads us to Chapel Road.

Here, viewed from the west, we see the chapel and refer once more to Baines' *"History of Lancashire"*: *"Formerly there were two dissenting chapels in this parish, but there is now only one, namely the Primitive Methodist chapel, which was built in 1827; the Independent preaching-room having been closed, after existing about eight years".*

The present chapel, built on adjacent land and standing further back from the road, replaced the original one in 1938. Other changes are that the white properties, central to the photograph, have been demolished to make way for the *"Glen Park Drive"* development.

On leaving Chapel Road and turning right along Shore Road we arrive at the *'Day School'*, which in 1919 was the gathering place prior to the Hesketh Bank Peace Parade. This school – now the primary school – has been greatly extended and modernised.

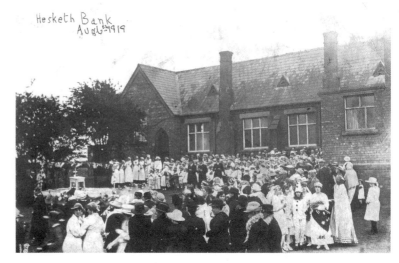

These photographs of the parade are virtually self explanatory, but looking more closely at the participants it is pleasing to see a special section devoted to nurses, who must have played an essential part in the war, with the decorated horse-drawn lorry depicting *"Britannia and her Dominions"* – again a fitting tribute to our allies.

Proceeding along Shore Road we pass Guide Road to our left, and with the natural north-easterly boundaries of the Rivers Ribble and Douglas we pause to reflect on the varied crossings of the rivers in times past.

The first recorded hostelry for travellers across the Ribble in the 1100's, was at Ball's Farm. Due to the vagaries of the channel, in the 1200's the route of the Ribble changed – being 2-3 miles wide – a guide being then necessary for travellers to cross with safety between Hesketh Bank (Ribble Bank Farm) and Naze Point at Freckleton, hence *"Guide"* Road. Crossings of the River Douglas are recorded – to Longton *"Dolphin Inn"*, Hoole *"Marsh House Lane"* and *"Haunders Lane"*.

Moving onwards we round the corner – known locally as *"Big Brow"* – and with the exception of the farm and barn in the background, all these properties have now gone, making way for modern housing. Adjacent to the white property central to the photograph was a small thoroughfare quaintly named *"Titmouse"* – the developers have chosen to re-name this area simply *"The Brow"*.

Continuing along Station Road towards the heart of the village, on the left are the sports fields and recreational centres, whilst on the right we pass *"The Grange"*, a substantial property still easily recognisable from this photograph.

As we approach and turn left into Becconsall Lane on this corner site stands the Parish Church of All Saints, the modern church hall and the recently constructed rectory. The foundation stone inside the church was laid by Lady Fermor-Hesketh on June 20th 1925, construction was complete by the following May and the service of consecration took place on July 9th 1926.

Formerly the home of the Lord of the Manor, on the left and standing well back from the road is *"Becconsall Hall"*.

Another interesting item of local history is that *"William Fleetwood"* an eminent lawyer and Recorder of London in 1569 was born in Becconsall. He died in 1592, after having distinguished himself by several published and manuscript works, a quote of the time being *"... he was a learned man and a good antiquarian"*.

Pictured here is *"Ferry House"*. The last person to live here whilst being in charge of the ferry to Hoole was Mrs Wareing, who used a punt for the crossing. It is said that she always wore a *'brat'* (apron) under which she kept a truncheon for use if the customer refused to pay the one penny fare!

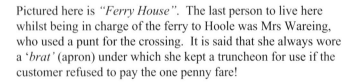

"*Becconsall Old Church of All Saints*" has stood on this spot since the mid 18th century at a time when – as recounted by a villager – the worshippers of Tarleton and Hesketh Bank could not agree, the Tarleton people at that time attending St. Mary's Church. In the time of Archdeacon Fletcher at Tarleton a new pulpit was installed in their Holy Trinity church, the old one being transferred to the superseded church of St. Mary. As a gesture of friendship the spare pulpit from St. Mary's was donated to Becconsall Church (a much poorer parish at that time with no proper pulpit); this pulpit went on the move again when it was considered that the church would be demolished, but once more refitted in the late 1900's when the "*Churches Conservation Trust*" took over the responsibility for its maintenance, together with a local fund-raising group, ensuring its future use for such events as exhibitions and lectures.

A more serious threat to it came during WWII when a stray enemy bomb caused shrapnel damage to its west wall and gravestones, amongst which is one marking the burial place of a river guide by the name of Thomas Blundell, who met his end on 6th July 1844 at the age of 58. His obituary ends with these words:

> "*Often times I have crofs'd the sands*
> *And through the Ribble deep;*
> *But I was found in Asland drown'd*
> *Which caused me here to sleep.*
> *It was God's will it should be so,*
> *Some way or other all must go.*"

Our villages continually give us an ever-changing landscape – in 1926, at the end of Hall Carr Lane, Walmer Bridge, it was with shovel and sweat. It is interesting to look back at how things used to be, but as we reminisce, we also realise how important it is to document these changes for the benefit of our children and grandchildren – one day it will be their turn.

Sadly, despite asking several local people and hours of simply searching, we were unable to locate these properties – believed to be in the Tarleton / Hesketh Bank area. Either they are no longer standing or they have been altered to such an extent that recognition is impossible. Maybe you know differently?